WHOSE MONEY IS IT?

Five Reasons Why You Can't Hold On To It

M. E. MARSHALL

Copyright © 2016 by GRACE Publishing Incorporated

All rights reserved. No part of this publication may be reproduced, distributed, or transmitted in any form or by any means, including photocopying, recording, or other electronic or mechanical methods, without the prior written permission of the publisher, except in the case of brief quotations embodied in critical reviews and certain other noncommercial uses permitted by copyright law. For permission requests, write to the publisher, addressed "Attention: Permissions Coordinator," at the address below.

GRACE Publishing Incorporated
PO Box 882
Duluth, GA. 30096
www.grace2014.wix.com/gracepublishinginc

Ordering Information:
Quantity sales. Special discounts are available on quantity purchases by corporations, associations, and others. For details, contact the publisher at the address above.
Printed in the United States of America

Cover Design by Tywebbin Creations LLC

Publisher's Cataloging-in-Publication data
Marshall, M.E.
Whose Money Is It? Five Reasons Why You Can't Hold On To It?
ISBN 9978-0-9972576-1-8

1. The main category of the book —Faith Religion. 2. Finance —From one perspective.
First Edition

All scripture quotations, unless otherwise noted, are taken from the New International Version "NIV" Copyright © 1973, 1978, 1984, by International Bible Society. Used by permission of Zondervan. All rights reserved.

Table of Contents

Acknowledgements	5
Introduction	7
Reason One	
Matters of the Heart	9
Matters of the Heart – Bible Study Lesson	13
Reason Two	
What's Your Focus?	17
What's Your Focus? - Bible Study Lesson	21
Reason Three	
Is Greed Good or Bad?	25
Is Greed Good or Bad? - Bible Study Lesson	29
Reason Four	
What Do You Treasure?	33
What Do You Treasure? – Bible Study Lesson	37
Reason Five	
Can You Recognize The Idols In Your Life?	41
Can You Recognize the Idols in Your Life? - Bible Study Lesson	45
Conclusion	49
Biblical References	51
Resources	59

Acknowledgements

This bible study workbook is a labor of love. Love first and foremost for my Heavenly Father. Secondly for my brothers and sisters in Christ and certainly, not to exclude those who are lost and struggling, desiring to experience a better quality of life.

Writing this book has been a journey. All praise and gratitude is rightfully given to God; He divinely orchestrated the events that resulted in the launching of G.R.A.C.E. Financial Ministry.

This mission began many years ago; in a small Baptist church in Georgia, 30 miles north of Atlanta. Having worked in the field of Credit and Collections for many years it only seemed natural my first volunteer role would be serving in the church's Finance Ministry. Quickly, I realized I had developed a passion for the role and seemingly, overnight I catapulted into a leadership role. I accepted responsibility for managing the finances of the church. A role I took very seriously. Honestly, I believed God gifted me with the passion: my heart's desire was to oversee His finances. I served in that role for over 13 years. It was during those years that I witnessed members of the congregation struggling in their finances. Sadly, I also witnessed in the secular environment, my co-workers were experiencing the same struggles. It was clear for me that the one thing both groups shared in common was a wrong perspective of their resources. This inspired the birth of G.R.A.C.E. Financial Ministry; G.R.A.C.E. is an acronym for God's Resources Advancing Christian Evangelism.

Over the years I've attended several conferences, read many great books on finances, facilitated small group studies which served to increase my understanding of what the Bible says about wealth, money and how He wants us (His children) to manage them. I also researched the needs of individuals at ground level, discovering what their concerns were related to finances and debt. This process confirmed that my knowledge and experience acquired from the jobs working in Finance, training received from workshops, church conferences and Biblical studies on leadership and money management could be of great benefit to those with need in this area. In a clear concise way, I began writing and developing curriculum I hoped would resonate with both Christians and non-believers. The finished product is what you are now holding in your hands, *"Whose Money Is It?"* I pray you are blessed by the material and truly acquire a profound understanding of God's resources.

Truthfully, I have been blessed to have a support team that holds me accountable, encourages and challenges me to excel. I am especially thankful for my spiritual parents and friends, Pastor (Poppy) Ervin A. and Jacquelyn Kimble. It was under the tutelage of Pastor Kimble that I learned how to study scripture accurately. I received a sound understanding of God's Word through his ministry teaching. Additionally, Pastor Kimble provided an environment whereby I was exposed to great teachers like Tony Evans, John Maxwell; including powerful ministries of the likes of Grace Ministries International, North American Missions Board and numerous others.

This list of individuals and organizations that have inspired and empowered me forward is not exhaustive. The sum total of those are too many to mention here; however, I can humbly and sincerely affirm, I am a much better person and my life is enriched because of the influence of each and every one.

Introduction

The first step in discovering "Whose Money Is It?" is to lay a solid foundation. It's essential to first get an understanding of how Christians **should** view their God given resources; time, talents and treasures. The reasons why most people do not act responsibly when it comes to their time, talent and treasures are numerous, however, the most significant reasons are listed here and unpacked throughout this reading. This study will address; ***Heart***, ***Focus***, ***Greed***, ***Treasure***, & ***Idols*** as the top contributing reasons why a great number of individuals are challenged in their finances. The stance taken in those areas will determine whether you are behaving as a good steward of what God has given you.

When you think concerning your time, talent and treasure has it every occurred to you that how these areas of your life are managed will greatly impact how you manage the resources of God? God is the owner of everything; in the earth, on the earth, above the earth and beyond.

> Psalms 24:1-3 states; *"The earth is the LORD's, and everything in it, the world, and all who live in it; for he founded it on the seas and established it on the waters. Who may ascend the mountain of the LORD? Who may stand in his holy place?"*

Since everything belongs to the Lord that means we are not owners, just managers or stewards of what God has placed in our hands. A manager is responsible for and oversees property belonging to another. In the parable of the talents, Jesus uses the example of a manager giving talents, or a certain measure of money, to his servants based on their ability to manage the responsibility. As a point of reference, a talent was worth about 20 years of a day laborer's wages. So, imagine the responsibility of the one with the five talents compared to the one given only one talent.

> Matthew 25:15 says: *"And to one he gave five talents, to another two, and to another one, to each according to his own ability; and immediately he went on a journey."*

The idea here is God gives you, in this case talents, time, or treasures according to your ability to manage them until He returns. In verse 29 Jesus tells us:

> *"For to everyone who has, more will be given, and he will have abundance; but from him who does not have, even what he has will be taken away."*

When Deuteronomy 8:18b says *"But remember the Lord your God, for it is he who gives you the ability to produce wealth"*, we are told in no uncertain terms that not only did God create all things, and owns all things, it is He who gives us the ability to obtain wealth!

The view of the Old and New Testament is that wealth is a blessing from God. Abraham is a typical example of a wealthy God-fearing man (Genesis 13:2). The psalmists celebrate material blessings. The godly man flourishes 'like a tree planted by streams of water' (Psalms 1:3). 'Wealth and riches' are in the house of the man that 'fears the Lord' (Psalms 112:1, 3). God is beneficent, and material wealth is a consequence of His bounty: 'God … richly furnishes us with everything to enjoy' (1 Timothy 6:17)

So, let's see what hinders you from being a good manager!

Matters of the Heart

In Jeremiah 17:9 it states *"The heart is deceitful above all things and beyond cure. Who can understand it?"* The only answer to that question is God. We find the premise which substantiates God is the accurate answer in Romans 8:27 *"…he who searches our hearts knows the mind of the Spirit, because the Spirit intercedes for God's people in accordance with the will of God."*

What is your heart's desire? What do you consider to be of value to you? What is your heart's desire? What do you love? When asked these questions, more often, many have listed material possessions, respected position, power and influence and the approval of 'man'. These questions must be answered. Take a moment, what would be your responses? In researching the scriptures, 1Timothy 6:10 introduces the greatest competitor for our heartbeat, it states *"the love of money is the ROOT to ALL kinds of evil."* (*Emphasis added*) What do you think Paul is trying to convey to Timothy in this verse? In Matthew Henry's commentary of this passage, he summarized the congregants are endeavoring to have their religion work for them and their secular or earthly desires. Henry is stating that the truth 1Timothy is claiming is "godliness with contentment". (1Timothy 6:6)

This viewpoint is in stark contrast with the world's view of success and accomplishments. According to the dictionary, the definition of success is;

- ♥ The favorable and prosperous termination of attempts or endeavors
- ♥ The attainment of wealth, position, honors, or the like
- ♥ A successful performance or achievement
- ♥ A person or thing that is successful
- ♥ The accomplishment of an aim or purpose
- ♥ The attainment of popularity or profit

An article, *The Only Definition of Success That Matters* by Jeff Haden, states that "The happier you are, the more successful you are." Now we have introduced happiness! So, I pose the question; is being happy a biblical principle? How would you define the difference between happiness and joy? In Matthew 6:33, Jesus tells His followers to *"seek first the kingdom and His righteousness, and all "these" things will be given to you as well."* (*Emphasis added*) What do you think Jesus is referring to when He says *"these" things*? Jesus, who was giving His Sermon on the Mount, had just told the parable about storing up treasures in Heaven and admonishing the crowd not to worry about their needs; such as what to eat, drink or wear.

The people were concerned about their survival. They were under Roman rule, heavily taxed and many lived in poverty. I can imagine hearing of the promised Messiah presence in the land filled the people with expectancy of freedom and yes happiness, finally! They were broken hearted and discouraged. Judea came under direct Roman administration in 4 BC, creating animosity between the Jews and the Romans. They were ready to be rescued.

However, what Jesus was referring to wasn't physical treasure, it was spiritual treasurer. He wanted them to see that the pagans chased after those things; yet, as children of God they were privileged. If only they had faith to believe that God would provide for them as He did for the birds of the air. *"....your heavenly Father knows that you need them. But seek first the kingdom of God and His righteousness, and all these things shall be added to you".* (Matthew 6:32b -33) *"Take delight in the Lord, and he will give you the desires of your heart."* (Psalm 37:4) Wow imagine that! Receiving the desires of your heart gifted to you by the Most High, with His blessings!

Let's summarize what we have discovered:

- ♥ The heart is deceitful.
- ♥ The <u>love</u> of money is the root to all kinds of evil.
- ♥ God searches and knows our heart.
- ♥ The world defines success in terms of gains, wealth, position, popularity.
- ♥ Our heavenly Father knows what we need.
- ♥ If we seek Him, He will supply all our needs.

Earlier the question was poised regarding how you might distinguish Joy and Happiness. In Proverbs 21:15 it says *"When justice is done, it brings joy to the righteous but terror to evildoers."* Isaiah tells us that with joy we are to draw water from the wells of salvation. (Isaiah 12:3). Paul tells us in Romans to be joyful in hope, patient in affliction and faithful in prayer. (Romans 12:2) John wrote *"I have no greater joy than to hear that my children are walking in the truth"*. 3 John 1:4 John's reference was directed to his spiritual children; those who received his testimony about Jesus and believed in response, he had "no greater joy".

The dictionary defines "joy" as:

- ♥ The emotion of great delight or happiness caused by something exceptionally good or satisfying

- ♥ A source or cause of keen pleasure or delight
- ♥ The expression or display of glad feeling
- ♥ A state of happiness or felicity

But what about happiness, what does the dictionary say about that?

- ♥ The quality or state of being happy
- ♥ Good fortune; pleasure; contentment; joy

Joy is defined, by Webster's, as an **emotion.** In contrast, happiness is defined as a **state of mind**. John had no greater joy than seeing the outcome of what God was doing in the lives of those he had ministered to. An emotion is solely dependent upon some external presence or condition. If that external influence is positive, you will experience a positive emotion, however, if that external influence is negative, the result will be a negative emotion, resulting in the loss of the opportunity to experience joy! Joy is conditional by the world's standard.

Paul and Silas were chained in prison for casting out a "familiar spirit" from a female slave who proclaimed the living Christ, but only for a profit to her owners. Paul and Silas definitely experienced negative external influences, but their response was to sing praises to the Lord! (Romans 16:16-28) Despite their circumstances, they had joy, an internal spiritual joy.

The prisons in Roman biblical times were often; underground, empty cisterns or wells. It was common place for prisoners to die from diseases caused by overcrowding. Many prisoners died in custody from starvation, beatings, or suicide. It was not a place to have joy, or to sing. It was miserable, dark, cold, and damp! How did Paul and Silas react to their situation and surroundings? Was it Negative or Positive? Read Acts 16:25 and I will allow you to be the judge.

Now let's turn our attention to happiness. The dictionary says happiness is a state of mind. Paul admonishes new Christians to "renew their minds" in Romans 12:2;

"Do not conform to the pattern of this world, but be transformed by the renewing of your mind. Then you will be able to test and approve what God's will is—his good, pleasing and perfect will." (Emphasis added)

Having a renewed mind means having the mind of Christ! 1 Corinthians 2:16 says *"for, Who has known the mind of the Lord so as to instruct him? But we have the mind of Christ"*.

So, what is the conclusion of the matter of the heart? God wants your heart, not your money or possessions. He wants a relationship with you and He made that possible through the life, death, and resurrection of His Son. When you are in love with that special someone, you want to spend every waking moment with him or her, correct? Your desire is to get to know them; their favorite foods, colors, sports team, perfume/cologne, hobbies, anything, and everything. You seek to please the love of your life, true? You don't avoid or hide from them. No, just the opposite, you call or text often, just to let them know you are thinking about them. Considering that you probably spend a great deal of time doing just that! This is a description of what it looks like when a person has your heart! And out of your relationship you most likely have their heart. How much more should God have your heart if you truly love Him and are His child? Psalm 19:14 sums it all up,

> *"Let the words of my mouth and the meditation of my heart Be acceptable in Your sight, O Lord, my strength and my Redeemer"*.

Your spending decisions will be impacted as a result of the relationship you form with God through His Son Jesus Christ. Your value is not calculated in computing your material possessions. Your connection to your Heavenly Father, embracing His everlasting love and applying the knowledge of His Holy word brings you immeasurable valuable.

Matters of the Heart – Bible Study Lesson

Introduction

What do you consider to be of value to you? What is your heart's desire? What do you love? Is it material possessions, position, and/or the approval of "man"? According to 1 Timothy 6:10, *"the love of money is the <u>ROOT</u> to <u>ALL</u> kinds of evil"*. (*Emphasis added*) Notice Paul isn't saying money itself is evil as some extremist claim. It's the value or allegiance placed on the money that causes the sinful desire. In v9 it says *'But those who desire to be rich fall into temptation and a snare, and into many foolish and harmful lusts which drown men in destruction…"* Read 1 Timothy 6:6-10

According to Matthew Henry's commentary; the congregants were endeavoring to have their religion work for them <u>***AND***</u> their secular desires. Henry points out the truth being projected in this passage is "godliness with contentment". (1Timothy 6:6)
- ♥ How do you interpret what Paul is conveying?
- ♥ How has this passage impacted your value system?
- ♥ What is your perception of what society deem is valuable?

We began this chapter referencing Jeremiah 17:9: *"The heart is deceitful above all things and beyond cure. Who can understand it?"* The New King James translation terms the heart as being 'wicked' as opposed to deceitful. The beginning of understanding whose money is it, begins with focusing on the condition of the heart. What has your heart? Rather, the true question is who has your heart? The answer to these questions will assist you in understanding the condition of your heart and will substantiate why and how you make your spending decisions.

Read Jeremiah 17:1-10 and answer the following questions

1. Why is Jeremiah saying the heart is deceitful?

_____
_____
_____

2. In your own words, write a brief synopsis OR summary of your interpretation of this passage?

_____
_____
_____

Read Romans 8:27

3. Does this verse answer Jeremiah's question?

4. How would you respond?

5. Does being happy equal being contented?

6. Does joy come because of happiness, or is it based on something more significant?

Read 3 John 1:4

7. Who is talking in this passage? Who is the audience?

Read Psalm 37:4

8. What do you understand from this verse should be your first priority?

When you think about joy, what comes to mind? Joy is defined, by Webster's, as an emotion but what is joy according to the Bible?

Read Act 16:25

9. Finding yourself in circumstances outlined in this scripture, would you have joy?

_____

_____

_____

10. The outer rim of the heart below reflects what you show to others; the next inner layer is what your family and friends see; and the center reflects your relationship with God, your '*Heart*'. Color the areas of the heart where you are being a good steward. The uncolored areas will reveal your opportunity to improve. This is not to cause you condemnation; yet, an opportunity to perform a self-assessment and purpose to grow in these areas.

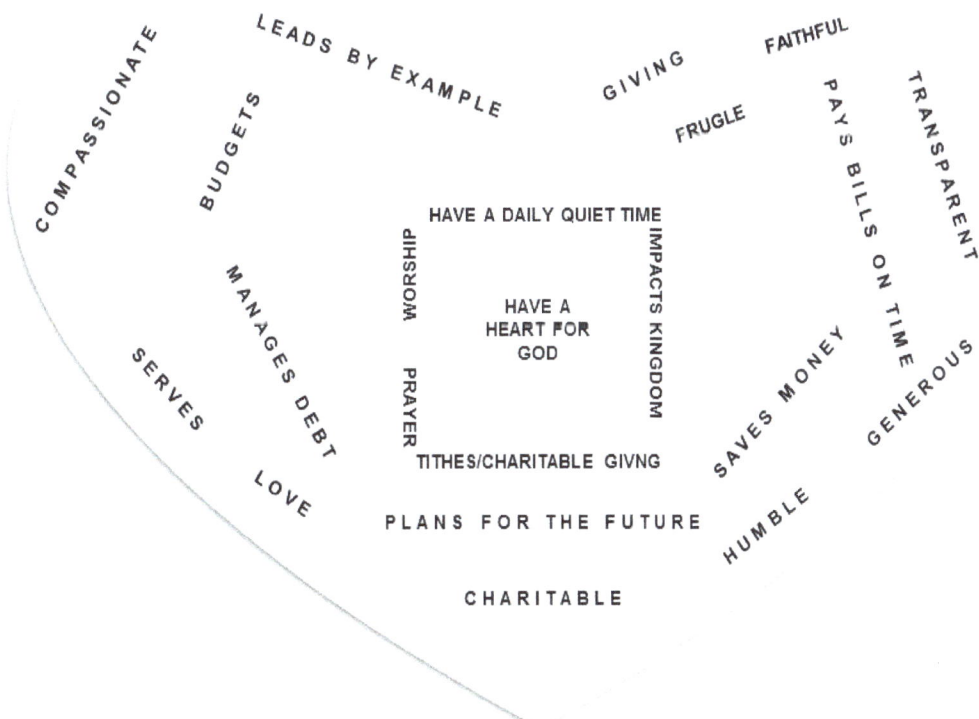

What's Your Focus?

What do you think about during the day? What thoughts occupy your mind? What has your undivided attention? Is it the report or presentation you promised your boss? Is it the next vacation trip or social event? Could it be a wayward child or a relationship challenge that is pressing on your heart? Is it a special program at your local church that you are preparing to facilitate? Whatever it is, perhaps, it has your complete focus. Throughout Psalm 86, David, the author, pleads for the Lord to hear and acknowledges his needs. He prays for an undivided heart, other versions translate "unite my heart". David's primary focus was on being in right standing with the God of the universe. David was anointed to be the next king of Israel succeeding Saul. Although, considerable time passed from the point of David's anointing, until he would actually take the throne.

David was a young man, 20 years old, when he defeated Goliath honoring Saul and the army of the living God. Driven by insecurity, disobedience and jealousy, Saul eventually had a change of heart towards David pursuing him with vengeance to kill him. An excerpt from The New Bible Dictionary Third Edition provides further insight: "Once Saul was dead, David sought the will of God and was guided to return to Judah, his own tribal region. Here his fellow-tribesmen anointed him king, and he took up royal residence in Hebron. He was then 30 years old......David's long reign was to last for 33 years". (Jones, T. H)

David fled from Saul, and later from Absalom, his own son. If anyone could justify being focused on self, or their own issues, it would have been David.

There are so many distractions in the high-tech world you live in today. Friends, family, and children, as much as you love them, can pull you away from spending time with God. Additionally, smartphones; tablets, laptops, and social media connections, all provide the opportunity to challenge your attention and focused away from the things of God or time with God. Daily attempts to capture your attention start from the moment you get out of bed in the morning. If you turn on the television to watch the morning news; you will have advertisers constantly vying for our attention offering to sell you everything from aspirin to Zumba classes. On the drive to work, listening to the radio; morning talk show hosts offer commentary on the most recent celebrity or political news. Complete with their opinion; and often extend you an opportunity for you to phone in to offer your 'expert' opinion as well. There is always a local and national news story which tends to evoke alarm and causing you to wonder, what is happening in the world today?

Upon arrival at work you are faced with the preverbal 'water cooler' conversation about either last night's sports game, or what's happening with the "Housewives", or another hot topic TV show. Let's not forget the overloaded e-mail inbox, video conferencing, and idle conversations with passing co-workers. These to name a few of the many things that are distracting and challenge your thought life. Now, I pose the question, when do you take the time to think about the things of God? It is easy to see why your attention can easily be divided? Romans 8:5-6 states;

> *"Those who live according to the flesh have their minds set on what the flesh desires; but those who live in accordance with the Spirit have their minds set on what the Spirit desires. The mind governed by the flesh is death, but the mind governed by the Spirit is life and peace."*

I have a female lab/shepherd mix named Brownie. She's 9 years old, weighs approximately 80lbs but still thinks she's a puppy weighing only 20lbs. Brownie, in my opinion, has Attention Deficit Disorder (ADD). The reason I believe this to be true, is because when I take her outside to relieve herself, any little thing easily distracts her. It could be; another dog, a squirrel, the wind, or a sound. It takes very little to cause her to lose focus. When she is distracted it takes several minutes to regain her focus and back on track to her purpose for being out there.

Honestly, I believe some Christians are similarly distracted, tending to easily lose their focus. Yet, their ADD is not the term as diagnosed by medical profession, but simply '**_A Detour in Direction_**' (ADD). God has a plan for each of us. He has assignments or commands and requirements for each of us to fulfill. (Jeremiah 29:11) In Exodus, the Israelites continued to disobey the Lord's commands. In the 16th chapter the Lord provided manna (food) at the request of the people. He gave specific instructions on how to gather the manna each day. However, the people either out of a lack of faith or greed gathered and stockpiled more than they should. The next day it was spoiled. They expected that it would be usable anytime they wanted (Exodus 16:15-20)

The people were continually trying to meet their own needs; failing to see all the while God had already made provisions for their every need. All that was required from the children of

Israel was to obey God's command. Exodus 16:28 *"Then the Lord said to Moses, "How long will you refuse to keep my commands and my instructions?"*

The same question is being asked of us today, how long will we refuse to acknowledge Him, and keep His commands. God commands His children to give a tenth of all their increase to Him, in a tithe. (Malachi 3:8) In doing so God promises to open the window of Heaven and pour out a blessing. By being obedient, in tithing, God can make the remaining 90% be more than sufficient to meet every need. For the records, the tithe did not originate from the Mosaic Law, or from the New Testament. Abraham offered a tenth of the goods taken in battle, in thankfulness to God for victory. Read the account in Genesis 14:18-20.

God commands us to be obedient not only in deeds, but in thought as well. In 2 Corinthians 10:5-6 Paul provides us with the tools to be able to be obedient;

> *"We demolish arguments and every pretension that sets itself up against the knowledge of God, and we take captive every thought to make it obedient to Christ. And we will be ready to punish every act of disobedience, once your obedience is complete"*.

You are to take captive every thought and I would also suggest every deed. The dictionary's definition for captive is;

- ♥ A person who is enslaved or dominated
- ♥ Made or held prisoner,
- ♥ Kept in confinement or restraint
- ♥ Pertaining to a captive

Many types of thoughts would be considered good thoughts. Inspirational reading from co-workers or acquaintances and spam e-mails are received almost daily. There are funny thoughts, motivational thoughts, thoughts for the day, positive thoughts etc. These are not bad in and of themselves. In Proverbs 12:15 we are told, *"The way of a fool is right in his own eyes, but he who listens to counsel is wise."* One of Webster's definitions for fool is; a person who lacks judgment or sense.

Ok, so you can get off focus from the things of God, but now the question is why? Why do some put God on the back burner, or maybe only think about Him on Sunday's if at all? In the Old Testament, after the Israelites were delivered from Pharaoh by Moses, the Law was given. In Deuteronomy 11:18 it says *"Fix these words of mine in your hearts and minds; tie them as symbols on your hands and bind them on your foreheads*". The two key words in this text that should stand out are "**hearts**" and "**minds**". We discussed the heart in the previous lesson, so let's look at the mind.

Going back to Webster's, mind is defined as;

- ♥ The element, part, substance, or process that; reasons, thinks, feels, wills, perceives, judges, etc.: "the processes of the human mind."
- ♥ Psychology - The totality of conscious and unconscious mental processes and activities.
- ♥ Intellect or understanding, as distinguished from the faculties of feeling and willing; intelligence.
- ♥ Reason, sanity, or sound mental condition

Basically, the mind is the part of the body that allows human beings to reason, think, feel, will etc. And according to our scripture from Deuteronomy, we are to "fix", or make a conscience decision to focus on God's words, or His Word, which is basically, the teachings of the Bible. How is that possible? The answer is found in James 1:22 *"Do not merely listen to the word, and so deceive yourselves. Do what it says….."*

James is challenging you to go a step further and don't just listen to or read the Word, yet to actually do what it says. That requires focus and making a conscience effort, which cannot be achieved by allowing the distractions of this world to overpower your thoughts. Let's revisit Paul, who tells us in Romans 12:2 *"And do not be conformed to this world, but be transformed by the renewing of your mind, that you may prove what is that good and acceptable and perfect will of God."* Being conformed simply means doing what everyone else is doing. By definition conformed means to; imitate, follow, adapt, or obey. In contrast, God is telling us through Paul not to do that, yet to be transformed, which means altered, changed, or converted.

I like to think we are called by God to be nonconformist. It means "a person who refuses to conform, as to established customs, attitudes, or ideas". Paul is telling Christians to refuse to accept the ideologies of this world, but to embrace the theology of God's world.

What's Your Focus? - Bible Study Lesson

Introduction

In Psalm 86 David prays for an undivided heart. He was challenged with distractions, although he realized where he put his focus made a great difference. David was anointed at an early age however years passed before he sat on the throne of Israel. If anyone had an opportunity to direct his attention on his circumstances on self or their own issues, it would be David.

- ♥ What do you think about during the day?
- ♥ What thoughts occupy your mind?
- ♥ What has your undivided attention?

There are so many distractions in the technology age that we live in today. So, when do we think about the things of God? What can you do to stay focused on God?

Read Romans 8:5-6

1. What does this scripture say to you about what should be your focus?

_____
_____
_____

Christians tend to suffer from ADD; **A *Detour in Direction*** and get off focus. God has a plan for each of us, and He has commands and requirements for us. In Exodus, the Israelite continued to disobey the Lord's commands. He gave specific instructions for gathering manna each day. However, the people, out of a lack of faith or greed, gathered more than they should it was spoiled the next day.

Read Exodus 16:16

2. Do you think the Israelites had a spiritual ADD (*A Detour in Direction*)?

_____
_____
_____

Read 2 Corinthians 10:5

3. In order to take your thoughts captive, what must you do?

_____
_____
_____

Read Proverbs 12:15

4. Does thinking good thoughts alone, allow you to take every thought & make it obedient to Christ?

_____
_____
_____

5. Clearly, we get off focus on the things of God. The question is why?

_____
_____
_____

6. Why do you sometimes put God on the back burner, and maybe only think about Him on Sundays if at all?

_____
_____
_____

Read Deuteronomy 11:18

Two key words in this text that stand out are "*hearts*" and "*minds*". Basically, the mind is the part of the body that allows human beings to reason, think, feel, will etc. And according to our scripture from Deuteronomy, we are to fix, or make a conscience decision to focus on God's Words, or His 'Word", which is the Bible and its teachings.

7. What prevents you from focusing on God's Word?

_____

_____

_____

Read Colossians 3:1-3

8. What do you think Paul is stating here?

_____

_____

_____

Read Romans 12:2

9. What does being conformed mean? What are some examples of how you confirm to this world?

_____

_____

_____

10. What will you do to keep your mind focused on the things of God?

_____

_____

_____

Read 2 Chronicles 7:14

11. What does this passage say to you?

_____

_____

_____

Is Greed Good or Bad?

In the 1987 movie Wall Street, starring Michael Douglas, his character, Gordon Gekko's famous speech included: "The point is ladies and gentlemen that greed, for lack of a better word, is good. Greed is right, greed works. Greed clarifies, cuts through, and captures the essence of the evolutionary spirit. Greed, in all of its forms; greed for life; for money; for love, and knowledge has marked the upward surge of mankind". I submit that what Mr. Gekko is saying in this statement is; it is healthy for people to aspire to something more, to want more, to gain a better position, and be willing to do whatever it takes to accomplish that goal. It's the greed that promotes the "*whatever it takes*" characteristic that is the topic of this section. Then, adding to greed we will examine motivation, which is directly related to the heart's desire.

What does the Bible say about greed? Considering two passages, we find greater insights:

>Psalm 10:3 "*For the wicked boasts of his heart's desire; He blesses the greedy and renounces the Lord*"
>
>Proverbs 1:19 "*Such are the paths of all who go after ill-gotten gain; it takes away the life of those who get it*".

We have learned that the Bible has a lot to say about greed, the cause of it and the result of what greed produces. Curiously, Webster's definition is limited;

- Excessive or rapacious desire, especially for wealth or possessions

Rapacious, now that's an SAT word! One of its meanings is 'inordinately greedy; predatory; extortionate'. I would venture to say that would adequately describe Douglas' character, Mr. Gekko. Other synonyms are; greedy, voracious (another SAT word), gluttonous, ravenous, and insatiable. These words do not sound very noble; nothing like those so passionately and eloquently stated in the movie by Gordon Gekko. Greed sounds rather crude and selfish. Yes, selfish! Of course, this is in stark contrast to the Word of God. Jesus tells us if we are to follow Him, we are to deny ourselves.

In Matthew 16:24 Jesus says; "*If anyone desires to come after Me, let him deny himself, and take up his cross, and follow Me*". Later in 1 John 2:15 John repeats Jesus' words when he says; "*Do not love the world or anything in the world. If anyone loves the world, love for the*

Father is not in them." And John 12:25 puts it this way; "*Anyone who loves their life will lose it, while anyone who hates their life in this world will keep it for eternal life.*"

The Bible speaks of greed having a negative impact on one's life, here in this present age and for eternity. The Bible also says it's wicked, disqualifying an individual from serving in a position of Pastor or Deacon. Paul instructs Timothy when looking for church leader's in 1 Timothy they should; "*not given to wine, not violent, <u>not greedy for money</u>, but gentle, not quarrelsome, not covetous*". (*Emphasis added*) Yet, the question at hand is why are some people greedy or selfish or both? The character, Mr. Gekko, was clearly interested in wealth and power, at all costs.

What motivates the average person to be greedy for wealth or possessions, as in Webster's definition? One such answer could be having the wrong perspective. Measuring their value from other people's perspective or the accumulation of material possessions rather than from God and His redemptive work through His Son on the Cross.

From my perspective, I believe because of our sin nature, human beings are inherently selfish. There is a saying by British poet Samuel Butler, "Self-preservation is the first law of nature". If self-preservation is the first law of nature, I offer greed would be the second. We find the first example of self-preservation in the Garden of Eden. What was Adam's disclaimer for justification of his disobedience; "*The woman whom You gave to be with me, she gave me of the tree, and I ate.*" (Genesis 3:12) Immediately the women defended self, blaming the serpent! However, in the end God held all accountable and each suffered the consequences of which the effects are still being experienced today.

Greed for money and status has been named as the cause of; broken and dysfunctional families, the decline of major corporations, countries, states, and the ultimate loss, the soul of man. The number one reported cause of divorce is money. According to an article in Huffington Post by Sonya Britt, a Kansas State University researcher; "Arguments about money [are] by far the top predictor of divorce." Britt further stated "It's not children, sex, in-laws or anything else. It's money -- for both men and women." Co-author of the article, Jeffrey Dew added, "Arguments about money may also stem from couples' deeply held beliefs about the purpose of money". It is interesting Dew declares "deeply held beliefs" when describing the source of the conflict about money.

All too often men and now women work an average of 80 hours per week; leaving little time available to spend with their family, especially children. In this highly technical world, there are, smartphones, tablets, laptops, video conferencing, Bluetooth, Skype and much more, all designed to draw you deeper in the proverbial loop. There was a song in the 60's called The Cat's in the Cradle sung by Harry Chapman. I always thought it to be sad even so, I find the lyrics to be but a very telling story. Below is an excerpt from the lyrics:

My child arrived just the other day
He came to the world in the usual way
But there were planes to catch and bills to pay
He learned to walk while I was away
And he was talkin' 'fore I knew it, and as he grew
He'd say "I'm gonna be like you, Dad
You know I'm gonna be like you"

There are other verses in this song; however, the ending verses speak volumes relative to the examples that we are leaving for our children that are being played out in our present-day culture.

I've long since retired, my son's moved away
I called him up just the other day
I said, "I'd like to see you if you don't mind"
He said, "I'd love to, Dad, if I can find the time
You see my new job's a hassle and kids have the flu
But it's sure nice talking to you, Dad
It's been sure nice talking to you"
And as I hung up the phone it occurred to me
He'd grown up just like me
My boy was just like me

What legacy are you leaving for your children? What examples have you set for them to follow? Are you exemplifying for them that family truly matters, or are you showing them that greed supersede family?

What about corporations that dissolve and fail because of the greed of its top executives? We all remember the scandals surrounding the demise of Enron, WorldCom, and many others. Enron was guilty of inflating revenue by $586 million from 1997 until 2001. According to an article in The New York Times, "the company set aside $1.5 million for the 2001 Christmas party". Employees were given free laptops, office lunches at Houston's, an exclusive area restaurant, lavish vacations, cars, you name it; the sky was the limit. The earnings on that level did not exist; it was all a façade to create an illusion! And, the primary culprit was greed!

What about the soul of the person? How does greed affect 'man'? In Luke 11:39, Jesus answers that question, He says; "*Now you Pharisees make the outside of the cup and dish clean, but your inward part is full of greed and wickedness*." Jesus was speaking about the motivation and the heart of the Pharisees. They were more concerned with appearances and how the people saw them, rather than the things of God. Incidentally, the origin of the term Pharisee comes from the Aramaic word פרש (prsh), which means: to separate, divide, or distinguish.

Let's revisit 1Timothy 6:10, "*For the love of money is a root of all kinds of evil, for which some have strayed from the faith in their greediness, and pierced themselves through with many sorrows*." Strayed from the faith and pierced themselves through with many sorrows, that is a mouthful. According to the Asbury Bible Commentary what Paul is intending to do with this passage is to "characterize the opponents of the Gospel and the confusion of godliness with financial gain".

Sadly, in today's culture, many people calling themselves Christians suffer from this same fate. Howbeit, current day terminology camouflages it as "*Prosperity Gospel*".

Is Greed Good or Bad? - Bible Study Lesson

Introduction

What causes greed? Is it a sincere desire to achieve success and prominence gone badly? Is it fueled by our sin nature, materialism, and selfishness, or what? The ideals expressed by Michael Douglas' character, Gordon Gekko in the movie, Wall Street, continue to be conveyed in many different and colorful ways in our current day. It's been nearly 30 years since Wall Street opened in theaters around the country. If you are familiar with the movie, (using the concepts of the movie as a barometer) where do you land on the greed meter? How does it compare to those in Jesus' day?

Read Matthew 19:15-22

1. Based on this chapter, how would you say the young man felt about wealth?

___

Read Matthew 19:23

2. Why did Jesus say it was hard for a rich person to enter into the kingdom of Heaven?

___

Read Luke 12:13-19

3. Jesus is asked to divide an inheritance amongst the heirs. How would you describe the mindset of the heir initiating Jesus involvement with his brother to divide the inheritance?

___

4. How would you define the rich man in this parable?

___

5. Have you ever had thoughts or can you relate to the rich man or the brother wanting to split the inheritance?

___
___
___

6. Read Luke 12:16-20

In this story, the rich man was greedy for more. What were the consequences of his greed and what does God say about the man's actions?

___
___
___

7. Read 1 Timothy 6:6-10

There is a saying, the one with the most toys wins the game, but is that a true statement from your perspective? What are your thoughts on what makes you content? Is it internal or external?

___
___
___

8. Read Proverbs 23:17

Society today puts a value on what a person wears, the car they drive, or the house or neighborhood in which they live. It is likely there are many that are wealthy who are not believers, and live very extravagant lives. With the light of Proverbs 23:17 shining on the lives of much of the wealthy, would you say envy is one cause of greed?

___
___
___

9. Read Ecclesiastes 5:13

Solomon, the wisest and richest man in the world implies wealth can cause the owner harm. How did it cause him harm? Has money caused you harm and in what way?

_____

_____

_____

10. Do you have to be rich for money to cause harm?

_____

_____

_____

What Do You Treasure?

When you think of treasure, what comes to your mind? I think of chests full of gold coins and jewelry. Pirates, boats, Captain Hook, and eye patches. You may or may not share this same imagery, however, I offer whatever pattern your thoughts follow when you think in terms of treasure, it is usually related to something of great value. There are many scriptural references to the term 'treasure'. In the King James Version (KJV) of the Bible, the word 'treasure' is found 78 times. Its use has references to money, affection, possessions, and/or something of value. Jesus referred to the "Kingdom of Heaven" as a treasure. He often began His teachings with "The Kingdom of Heaven is like………a treasure in a field……….a man who sowed good seed in his field……….a mustard seed……….a merchant looking for fine pearls………etc. What is Jesus saying about treasures? True treasures are spiritual not physical.

According to the scriptures, the 'treasures' we should seek are found in the things of God, not in material possessions. You can treasure a moment an experience and a memory or a relationship, my point here is that what you treasure does not have to relate to a tangible thing of earthly value. Let's look at a definition of treasure:

- ♥ Wealth or riches stored or accumulated, especially in the form of precious metals, money, jewels, or plate.
- ♥ Anything or person greatly valued or highly prized
- ♥ To regard or treat as precious; cherish.
- ♥ To put away for security or future use, as money

Does your definition of treasure differ from God's? In Exodus God rescued His people the Israelites from slavery, under Pharaoh in Egypt, using Moses as His deliverer. In Exodus 19:5, God's speaks to His people through Moses and says *"Now therefore, if you will indeed obey My voice and keep My covenant, then you shall be a <u>special treasure</u> to Me above all people; for all the earth is Mine."* (*Emphasis added*) Imagine being a "special treasure" to God, the Creator of ALL things! Job treasured the Word of God, in Job 23:12 he says *"I have not departed from the commandment of His lips; I have <u>treasured</u> the words of His mouth More than my necessary food."* (*Emphasis added*) Job valued his obedience to God, more than life sustaining food.

Let's be honest, when treasure is mentioned in a church setting, most often, it is being referred to as money. Christians are admonished to utilize our Time, Talents, & Treasure (money) for the furthering of the gospel of Jesus Christ. So, the fact that treasure is defined as wealth, money, or something of value is not to be interpreted as a bad thing. God even says in His Word in Deuteronomy 8:18a *"And you shall remember the Lord your God, for it is He who gives you power to get wealth"*. Your wealth comes from God. He empowered you to create wealth; therefore, this can't be a bad thing. God gives you treasures, but not merely for yourself; although, you will reap the benefits as a byproduct. God intended that you would use your treasures for others; furthering His Kingdom agenda and to support others.

Where people get into trouble is when the material treasure(s) overshadows their relationship with Jesus Christ, and serving Him. The passage found in Mathew 6:21 and restated in Luke 12:34 makes a profound statement; *"For where your treasure is, there your heart will be also."*

At the start of this lesson I asked an important question, w*hen you think of treasure, what comes to your mind*? In other words, what do you value? Is it friends, family, your reputation, social status, position, or is it your relationship with the Most High God? The primary focus of this series is being a good steward of ALL of God's resources, and treasures. Yet, in the context of this study manual, it is referring to money, possessions and, things of monetary value, but only as it relates to your Godly focus. What does that look like?

In our lesson on *'What's Your Focus'* I mention King David's focus was on being in right standing with the God of the Universe. When thinking about monetary resources what would that look like in today's society? Let's suppose that God has blessed you with a 4-bedroom house, large rooms, with rich crown molding, and hardwood floors throughout, spacious master suite, a large back yard complete with wraparound deck and BBQ pit. There is plenty of room for guests to enjoy and to be very comfortable. If you are God focused, you would recognize, while it's great to have such a lovely home, it's not just for you.

You could possibly utilize your home to hosts Small Group Bible studies. Perhaps, invite those in your sphere of influence over for a BBQ and allow them insight to a godly home and to experience firsthand the interactions of a Christian family. In other words, present day witnessing. How you carry out God's call on your life, and He does have a call on your life, depends on your unique circumstances. (Jeremiah 29:11)

In Ephesians 1:11 is says;
"In him we were also chosen, having been predestined according to the plan of him who works out everything in conformity with the purpose of his will…"

What is God saying? It seems like He's telling us that He has a plan for our lives and those plans will work in accordance with the purposes of His Will, leaving no room for selfishness or greed.

Jesus told His disciples in Mathew 28:19

> *"Therefore go and make disciples of all nations, baptizing them in the name of the Father and of the Son and of the Holy Spirit, and teaching them to obey everything I have commanded you. And surely I am with you always, to the very end of the age*."

Now, we do not have to go any further than the next-door neighbor, the next office or cubicle and in some cases within our own homes to be a witness. We are cautioned by Peter; *"Always be prepared to give an answer to everyone who asks you to give the reason for the hope that you have. But do this with gentleness and respect…"* (1 Peter 3:15) This sounds as if someone has been prepared to give a testimony to me.

You may be pondering; I don't want to invite strangers into my home. Understandably, however, what about unsaved friends, family, or co-workers? Giving a testimony is nothing more than your telling the story of what God has done for you. God gives you resources, aka treasures, to accomplish this goal. Allow me to offer another example, your vehicle could be used to transport food or clothing to a shelter or a neighborhood cooperative. Look around your closets; those old suits, shoes, dresses, and slacks could be very useful when given to one of the many organizations that provide clothing for those re-entering the work force or underemployed and needing business appropriate attire. Also, consider providing clothing or blankets to homeless shelters in your community.

You truly are blessed, to be a blessing; to be a witness and a light in a dark world.

What Do You Treasure? – Bible Study Lesson

Introduction

Jesus said, "Where your treasure is, your heart will be also", but do you really believe that? Do you believe that what you value has your heart? If you value your car, does that mean that your car has your heart? Sounds ridiculous, doesn't it? But it's not just the car; it's what it represents, status, the envy of friends and family.

So, at the heart of the matter it could possibly be more an attitude towards the vehicle rather than a love affair with an inanimate object!

Read both Mathew 6:19 - 21 & Luke 12:32-34

Matthew speaks about the dangers of storing treasures on earth; being destroyed by moth and rust. Luke says to sell your treasures and give to the poor.

1. Given these two perspectives, what is God saying about treasures?

_____

_____

_____

Read Exodus 19:1-6

The Israelites had witnessed some powerful and amazing things; the locust, frogs, water turned to blood, the parting of the Red Sea so they could cross on dry land. The Mediterranean Sea, or Red Sea, provides a conduit south through the Suez Canal and Gulf of Suez. This salty sea is just over 190 miles (300 km) across at its widest point, and about 1,200 miles (1,900 km) in length. There's a measured maximum depth of 8,200 feet (2,500 m), and an estimated average depth of 1,640 feet (500 m). Much of the immediate shoreline is quite shallow.

2. What do you think caused them to doubt and want to go back to Egypt?

_____

_____

_____

3. Have you ever trusted in your own resources rather depend on God?

_____
_____
_____

4. Do you have a relationship with God? If not all you have to do is ask Jesus to come into your life, accept His forgiveness and He will answer you with a resounding YES! (See the prayer for salvation in the Conclusion section)

_____
_____
_____

5. Which do you treasure or value most; your material possessions or your relationship with God?

_____
_____
_____

6. Having witnessed the miracles God performed, do you think the Israelites should have realized that God was on their side, and had already answered their prayers for deliverance?

_____
_____
_____

Read Deuteronomy 8:10-14

7. What is your '*Egypt*'; is it your job or career, your money, or possessions?

_____
_____
_____

8. What are you 'slave' to? Is it a television show, a drug or addicting habit, sex, people pleasing etc.?

_____

9. What is being asked and what is being promised?

10. What is your response?

Can You Recognize The Idols In Your Life?

We've come to the final lesson in Whose Money Is It! What a journey! We have discussed four of the *Five Reasons Why You Can't Hold on to It*. We discussed the *Heart* in lesson one, our *Focus* in lesson two, *Greed* in lesson three, *Treasures* in lesson four and in this lesson, we are going to discuss reason five: *Idols*.

You may not consider that people have idols in their lives in present. Many thinks that only happened in biblical times. But, I beg to differ. First, I believe it wise to establish a working definition of idols. Webster's definition of Idols:

- An image or other material object representing a deity to which religious worship is addressed.
- Bible - an image of a deity other than God. Or - the deity itself
- Any person or thing regarded with blind admiration, adoration, or devotion:
- A mere image or semblance of something, visible but without substance, as a phantom
- A figment of the mind; fantasy
- A false conception or notion; fallacy

My preference is the second bullet: "An image of a deity **OTHER** than God". That would cause one to research what does the Bible say about idols? Let's start with peeking at the 10 commandments.

The first three commandments have to do with our relationship with God. In Exodus 20:1-6;

> *"And God spoke all these words, saying: I am the* Lord *your God, who brought you out of the land of Egypt, out of the house of bondage. You shall have no other gods before Me. "You shall not make for yourself a carved image—any likeness of anything that is in heaven above, or that is in the earth beneath, or that is in the water under the earth; you shall not bow down to them nor serve them. For I, the* Lord *your God, am a jealous God, visiting the iniquity of the fathers upon the children to the third and fourth generations of those who hate Me, but showing mercy to thousands, to those who love Me and keep My commandments."*

God makes it quite clear that He has no intention of allowing His creation to have idols and if they should, consequences will follow. Let's fast forward to the current year. Based on the third bullet of Webster's definition listed above, "any person or thing regarded with blind admiration, adoration, or devotion". Now compare that to what God says in His Word; *"You shall have no other gods before Me"*; Would you agree with me that it is possible to for you to have idols in your life today?

If Christians are brutally honest, we must admit that yes, we do have the propensity to have idols in their lives presently. They may not be in the form of images, as described in the Bible, or some pagan worship ritual. We have become too sophisticated for that! No, idols in today's society are presented the form of things that are acceptable and can be even classified as good things; i.e., our jobs, our families, ministry work and yes, dare I say it, our money! The making of it, spending it and keeping it can become a source of idol worship in our lives.

Let's take a closer look as to see what that looks like. I will be transparent and offer myself in this example. My idols are computer games and particular television shows; my preference is the game Hidden Objects and any classic black and white westerns. For those of you that may be too young to have experienced this, television wasn't always in color! Honestly, I can spend hours watching westerns and playing games. Hours that could be spent being more productive and/or spending time in God's Word. My precious time could serve me well, spending an hour relaxing and enjoying my computer game or TV show, and then, refocusing by renewing my mind as Paul states. Or, studying to show myself approved or any number of things Christians are commanded to do on a daily basis. Honestly, I constantly have to remind myself that I am not to put anything before or above God. For some people, it's their jobs, working 80+ hours a week, not spending time with family or in God's Word. Finding that they are too busy or too tired to go for church and engage in fellowship with other believers. For others, it's working out, or exercising. Please note there is nothing wrong with taking care of your body. Yet, obsessing about your looks can easily be the makings of an idol.

Materialism, another idol, having the best or expensive: Michael Kors, Prada, Gucci, DKNY, or whatever it is, that you **HAVE** to have the latest and greatest of. And let's not talk about Apple, iPods, Kindles and all the other electronic gadgets we are being enticed to purchase daily by retailer and advertisers.

Please note: let me go on record as stating that classic westerns, computer games, working, exercising, caring about your looks, having the latest technology, or purchasing a designer item are not bad things, **_UNLESS,_** they are placed above or are in competition with God; that is when they have the potential to become idols. In 2 Kings 17:40-41 the Message Bible puts it this way:

> *But they didn't pay any attention. They kept doing what they'd always done. As it turned out, all the time these people were putting on a front of worshiping God, they were at the same time involved with their local idols. And they're still doing it. Like father, like son.*

This passage says the people were walking the fence, worshiping God on their terms instead of His terms. Don't we do that; don't we want our cake and eat it too?

What are some of those consequences that I mentioned earlier? God is a jealous God, He will allow your circumstances put you in a position where your focus is turned back on or toward Him. That job that you take great pride in from which you get great satisfaction, the company downsizes and eliminates your position; presenting you with plenty of time to focus on God. With your revenue stream reduced or removed completely, you must look to Him for His provisions. All that exercising you've been doing, you pull a muscle or suffer a severe strain and can't work out for several weeks. Those computer games and westerns I enjoy so much, the computer crashes and the games are lost, or access to the Internet connection is lost. God will draw your attention to Him, one way or another; He will not be ignored, or set aside.

If money is your idol, you could lose it due to an unexpected bill or some type of repair needed and unfortunately, even illness. The object of your affection, money, would then be used for something other than what you intended.

You are encouraged to tear down your idols and worship God only. Anything that sets itself above God will be brought down.

Isaiah 14:12-14 tells of the fallen angel:

> *"How you are fallen from heaven, O Lucifer, son of the morning! How you are cut down to the ground, You who weakened the nations! For you have said in your heart: '__I__ will ascend into heaven, __I__ will exalt my throne above the stars of God; __I__ will also sit on the mount of the congregation On the farthest sides of the north; __I__ will ascend above the heights of the clouds, __I__ will be like the Most High."* (Emphasis added)

Notice "*I*" is mentioned five (5) times in these passages. What do you say, I need to…I have to… I'm going to…my this or my that! It's all about you and what you want.

Pride is an idol, what did Webster's say; "A false conception or notion; fallacy". We are to worship God, with all our hearts, all our minds, all our souls, in doing this we will cast down every idol. Putting God first in all you do is how you tear down those idols. Spending time in His Word daily, having a quiet time, fellowshipping with other believers. Turn off the TV, unplug the phone, start seeing God in His creation, the flowers, trees, rivers, lakes, mountains, see the majesty of all He's created and thank Him, praise Him, worship Him, for He is worthy to be praised.

Can You Recognize the Idols in Your Life? - Bible Study Lesson

Introduction

Was Adam and Eve's sin the first sin, or was the first sin pride? Pride exalts oneself above God and others. What are the idols in your life? Be honest with yourself and with God. He already knows. It's up to you to identify them and then repent and remove them as God reveals them to you.

Read Romans 12:2

1. Are you conforming to the patterns of this world?

_____
_____
_____

2. If so, what can you do about it? What or who do you need to remove from your life?

_____
_____
_____

Read Psalm 115:4

3. What idols do we have in the 21st Century that could fit the description of silver and gold?

_____
_____
_____

4. Based on what you've learned so far in this series, how does God respond to being replaced by idols in any form?

_____
_____
_____

Read Daniel 4:28-32

5. What does this passage say about pride? To fully understand the story read the entire chapter. Early in the chapter King Nebuchadnezzar had a dream which Daniel interrupted.

Do you suppose the king forgot what was told to him?

_____
_____
_____

6. What would you say are some idols in your life today?

_____
_____
_____

7. What do you need to do to remove them?

_____
_____
_____

8. What can you do to prevent idols forming in your life?

_____
_____
_____

Read 2 Chronicles 7:14

9. What do you need to repent of concerning; your heart, your focus, greed, treasures, or idols?

_____
_____
_____

Read 2 Corinthians 6:16

10. What your response?

_____
_____
_____

Conclusion

This study is not meant to beat you up or condemn you. The Bible says there is no condemnation in Christ Jesus. (Romans 8:1) As the saying goes, we do better when we know better. Let's review:

- ♥ Watch where your Heart is
- ♥ Watch what you Focus on
- ♥ Watch and be aware of areas of Greed in your life
- ♥ Watch what you Treasure
- ♥ Watch what and who are your Idols

God doesn't want your money, He wants your heart, your obedience, your reverence. Christians are called to be different, unique, and special. If the trappings of this world have you in bondage, how can you be the best God wants you to be? Commit to honoring God and studying His Word and being a good steward of all He has given you.

Now if you are not a member of the Body of Christ none of this will make any sense to you. If you haven't asked Jesus to be the Lord of your life you can now by praying this simple prayer:

"Dear God, I want to be a part of your family. You said in Your Word that if I acknowledge that You raised Jesus from the dead and if I asked for forgiveness of my sins and accept Him as my Lord and Savior, I would be saved. So God, I now say that I believe that You raised Jesus from the dead and that He is alive and well. I accept Him now as my personal Lord and Savior. I accept the gift of salvation from sin right now. I am now saved from the penalty of sin. Jesus is my Lord. Jesus is my Savior.

Thank you, Father God, for forgiving me, saving me, and giving me eternal life with You. Amen!"

If you prayed this prayer for the first time, go tell another Christian. You will need to get connected with a Bible-based church and get to know the God of the Universe and your purpose for Him creating you. Welcome to the Family!!

Biblical References

Introduction

Psalms 24:1-3 - The earth is the LORD's, and everything in it, the world, and all who live in it; for he founded it on the seas and established it on the waters. Who may ascend the mountain of the LORD? Who may stand in his holy place?"

Matthew 25:15 - And to one he gave five talents, to another two, and to another one, to each according to his own ability; and immediately he went on a journey."

Matthew 25:29 - For to everyone who has, more will be given and he will have abundance; but from him who does not have, even what he has will be taken away."

Deuteronomy 8:18b - But remember the Lord your God, for it is he who gives you the ability to produce wealth,"

Genesis 13:2 - Abram had become very wealthy in livestock and in silver and gold

Psalms. 1:3 - That person is like a tree planted by streams of water, which yields its fruit in season and whose leaf does not wither— whatever they do prospers.

Psalms 112:1-3 - **1** Praise the Lord. Blessed are those who fear the Lord, who find great delight in his commands **2** Their children will be mighty in the land; the generation of the upright will be blessed. **3** Wealth and riches are in their houses, and their righteousness endures forever.

1 Timothy 6:17 - Command those who are rich in this present world not to be arrogant nor to put their hope in wealth, which is so uncertain, but to put their hope in God, who richly provides us with everything for our enjoyment.

Matters of the Heart

Jeremiah 17:1-10 - "Judah's sin is engraved with an iron tool, inscribed with a flint point, on the tablets of their hearts and on the horns of their altars. **2** Even their children remember their altars and Asherah poles beside the spreading trees and on the high hills. **3** My mountain in the land and your wealth and all your treasures I will give away as plunder, together with your high places, because of sin throughout your country. **4** Through your own fault you will lose the inheritance I gave you. I will enslave you to your enemies in a land you do not know, for you have kindled my anger, and it will burn forever."**5** This is what the Lord says: "Cursed is the one who trusts in man, who draws strength from mere flesh and whose heart turns away from the Lord. **6** That person will be like a bush in the wastelands; they will not see prosperity when it comes. They will dwell in the parched places of the desert, in a salt land where no one lives. **7** "But blessed is the one who trusts in the Lord, whose confidence is in him. **8** They will be like a tree planted by the water that sends out its roots by the stream. It does not fear when heat comes; its leaves are always green. It has no worries in a year of drought and never fails to bear fruit." **9** The heart is deceitful above all things and beyond cure. Who can understand it? **10** "I the Lord search the heart and examine the mind, to reward each person according to their conduct, according to what their deeds deserve."

Romans 8:27 - Now He who searches the hearts knows what the mind of the Spirit is, because He makes intercession for the saints according to the will of God.

3 John 3:4 - I have no greater joy than to hear that my children are walking in the truth.

Psalm 37:4 - Take delight in the Lord, and he will give you the desires of your heart

Acts 16:16-28 - **16** Once when we were going to the place of prayer, we were met by a female slave who had a spirit by which she predicted the future. She earned a great deal of money for her owners by fortune-telling. **17** She followed Paul and the rest of us, shouting, "These men are servants of the Most High God, who are telling you the way to be saved." **18** She kept this up for many days. Finally Paul became so annoyed that he turned around and said to the spirit, "In the name of Jesus Christ I command you to come out of her!" At that moment the spirit left her. **19** When her owners realized that their hope of making money was gone, they seized Paul and Silas and dragged them into the marketplace to face the authorities. **20** They brought them before the magistrates and said, "These men are Jews, and are throwing our city into an uproar **21** by advocating customs unlawful for us Romans to accept or practice." **22** The crowd joined in the attack against Paul and Silas, and the magistrates ordered them to be stripped and beaten with rods. **23** After they had been severely flogged, they were thrown into prison, and the jailer was commanded to guard them carefully. **24** When he received these orders, he put them in the inner cell and fastened their feet in the stocks.

25 About midnight Paul and Silas were praying and singing hymns to God, and the other prisoners were listening to them. **26** Suddenly there was such a violent earthquake that the foundations of the prison were shaken. At once all the prison doors flew open, and everyone's chains came loose. **27** The jailer woke up, and when he saw the prison doors open, he drew his sword and was about to kill himself because he thought the prisoners had escaped. **28** But Paul shouted, "Don't harm yourself! We are all here!"

1 Timothy 6:10 - For the love of money is a root of all kinds of evil, for which some have strayed from the faith in their greediness, and pierced themselves through with many sorrows

1 Timothy 6:6 - Now godliness with contentment is great gain

Matthew 6:33 - But seek first the kingdom of God and His righteousness, and all these things shall be added to you.

Matthew 6:32 - For after all these things the Gentiles seek. For your heavenly Father knows that you need all these things.

Proverbs 21:15 - It is a joy for the just to do justice, But destruction will come to the workers of iniquity.

Isaiah 12:3 - Therefore with joy you will draw water From the wells of salvation.

Romans 12:2 - And do not be conformed to this world, but be transformed by the renewing of your mind, that you may prove what is that good and acceptable and perfect will of God.

3 John 1:4 - I have no greater joy than to hear that my children walk in truth.

Acts 16:25 - But at midnight Paul and Silas were praying and singing hymns to God, and the prisoners were listening to them.

1 Corinthians 2:16 - For "who has known the mind of the Lord that he may instruct Him?" But we have the mind of Christ

Psalm 19:14 - Let the words of my mouth and the meditation of my heart Be acceptable in Your sight, O Lord, my strength and my Redeemer.

What's Your Focus?

Psalm 86:11 - Teach me your way, Lord, that I may rely on your faithfulness; give me an undivided heart, that I may fear your name."

Jeremiah 29:11 - For I know the plans I have for you, declares the Lord, plans to prosper you and not to harm you, plans to give you hope and a future.

Romans 8:5-6 - **5** Those who live according to the flesh have their minds set on what the flesh desires; but those who live in accordance with the Spirit have their minds set on what the Spirit desires. **6** The mind governed by the flesh is death, but the mind governed by the Spirit is life and peace.

Exodus 16:15-17; 19-20 - And Moses said to them, "This is the bread which the Lord has given you to eat. **16** This is the thing which the Lord has commanded: 'Let every man gather it according to each one's need, one omer for each person, according to the number of persons; let every man take for those who are in his tent.'" **19** And Moses said, "Let no one leave any of it till morning." **20** Notwithstanding they did not heed Moses. But some of them left part of it until morning, and it bred worms and stank.

Exodus 16:16 - Then the Lord said to Moses, "How long will you refuse to keep my commands and my instructions?

Malachi 3:7-9 - **7** Ever since the time of your ancestors you have turned away from my decrees and have not kept them. Return to me, and I will return to you," says the Lord Almighty. "But you ask, 'How are we to return?' **8** "Will a mere mortal rob God? Yet you rob me. "But you ask, 'How are we robbing you?' "In tithes and offerings. **9** You are under a curse—your whole nation—because you are robbing me.

Genesis 14:18-20 – **18** Then Melchizedek king of Salem brought out bread and wine; he was the priest of God Most High. **19** And he blessed him and said: "Blessed be Abram of God Most High, Possessor of heaven and earth; **20** And blessed be God Most High, Who has delivered your enemies into your hand." And he gave him a tithe of all.

2 Corinthians 10:5 - We demolish arguments and every pretension that sets itself up against the knowledge of God, and we take captive every thought to make it obedient to Christ.

Proverbs 12:15 - The way of a fool is right in his own eyes, but he who listens to counsel is wise.

Deuteronomy 11:18 - Fix these words of mine in your hearts and minds; tie them as symbols on your hands and bind them on your foreheads.

Colossians 3:1-3 - **1** Since, then, you have been raised with Christ, set your hearts on things above, where Christ is, seated at the right hand of God. **2** Set your minds on things above, not on earthly things. **3** For you died, and your life is now hidden with Christ in God.

Romans 12:2 - And do not be conformed to this world, but be transformed by the renewing of your mind, that you may prove what is that good and acceptable and perfect will of God.

2 Chronicles 7:14 - if my people, who are called by my name, will humble themselves and pray and seek my face and turn from their wicked ways, then I will hear from heaven, and I will forgive their sin and will heal their land.

Is Greed Good or Bad?

Matthew 19:16-22 - **16** Just then a man came up to Jesus and asked, "Teacher, what good thing must I do to get eternal life?" **17** "Why do you ask me about what is good?" Jesus replied. "There is only One who is good. If you want to enter life, keep the commandments." **18** "Which ones?" he inquired. Jesus replied, "'You shall not murder, you shall not commit adultery, you shall not steal, you shall not give false testimony, **19** honor your father and mother,' and 'love your neighbor as yourself.' **20** "All these I have kept," the young man said. "What do I still lack?" **21** Jesus answered, "If you want to be perfect, go, sell your possessions and give to the poor, and you will have treasure in heaven. Then come, follow me." **22** When the young man heard this, he went away sad, because he had great wealth.

Matthew 19:23 - Then Jesus said to his disciples, "Truly I tell you, it is hard for someone who is rich to enter the kingdom of heaven".

1 John 2:15 - Do not love the world or anything in the world. If anyone loves the world, love for the Father is not in them. 16 For everything in the world—the lust of the flesh, the lust of the eyes, and the pride of life—comes not from the Father but from the world.

Luke 12:13-19 - **13** Someone in the crowd said to him, "Teacher, tell my brother to divide the inheritance with me." **14** Jesus replied, "Man, who appointed me a judge or an arbiter between you?" **15** Then he said to them, "Watch out! Be on your guard against all kinds of greed; life does not consist in an abundance of possessions." **16** And he told them this parable: "The ground of a certain rich man yielded an abundant harvest. **17** He thought to himself, 'What shall I do? I have no place to store my crops.' **18** "Then he said, 'This is what I'll do. I will tear down my barns and build bigger ones, and there I will store my surplus grain. **19** And I'll say to myself, "You have plenty of grain laid up for many years. Take life easy; eat, drink and be merry."'

1 Timothy 6:6-10 - **6** But godliness with contentment is great gain. **7** For we brought nothing into the world, and we can take nothing out of it. **8** But if we have food and clothing, we will be content with that. **9** Those who want to get rich fall into temptation and a trap and into many foolish and harmful desires that plunge people into ruin and destruction. **10** For the love of money is a root of all kinds of evil. Some people, eager for money, have wandered from the faith and pierced themselves with many griefs.

Proverbs 23:17 - Do not let your heart envy sinners, But be zealous for the fear of the Lord all the day;

Ecclesiastes 5:13 - I have seen a grievous evil under the sun: wealth hoarded to the harm of its owners…

What Do You Treasure?

Mathew 6:19 - 21 - **19** "Do not store up for yourselves treasures on earth, where moths and vermin destroy, and where thieves break in and steal. **20** But store up for yourselves treasures in heaven, where moths and vermin do not destroy, and where thieves do not break in and steal. **21** For where your treasure is, there your heart will be also.

Luke 12:32-34 - **32** "Do not be afraid, little flock, for your Father has been pleased to give you the kingdom. **33** Sell your possessions and give to the poor. Provide purses for yourselves that will not wear out, a treasure in heaven that will never fail, where no thief comes near and no moth destroys. **34** For where your treasure is, there your heart will be also.

Exodus 19:1- 6 - **1** On the first day of the third month after the Israelites left Egypt—on that very day—they came to the Desert of Sinai. **2** After they set out from Rephidim, they entered the Desert of Sinai, and Israel camped there in the desert in front of the mountain. **3** Then Moses went up to God, and the Lord called to him from the mountain and said, "This is what you are to say to the descendants of Jacob and what you are to tell the people of Israel: **4** 'You yourselves have seen what I did to Egypt, and how I carried you on eagles' wings and brought you to myself. **5** Now if you obey me fully and keep my covenant, then out of all nations you will be my treasured possession. Although the whole earth is mine, **6** you will be for me a kingdom of priests and a holy nation.' These are the words you are to speak to the Israelites."

Deuteronomy 8:10-14 - **10** When you have eaten and are satisfied, praise the Lord your God for the good land he has given you. **11** Be careful that you do not forget the Lord your God, failing to observe his commands, his laws and his decrees that I am giving you this day. **12** Otherwise, when you eat and are satisfied, when you build fine houses and settle down, **13** and when your herds and flocks grow large and your silver and gold increase and all you have is multiplied, **14** then your heart will become proud and you will forget the Lord your God, who brought you out of Egypt, out of the land of slavery.

Can You Recognize The Idols In Your Life?

Exodus 20:1-6 And God spoke all these words, saying: **2** "I am the Lord your God, who brought you out of the land of Egypt, out of the house of bondage. **3** "You shall have no other gods before Me. **4** "You shall not make for yourself a carved image—any likeness of anything that is in heaven above, or that is in the earth beneath, or that is in the water under the earth; **5** you shall not bow down to them nor serve them. For I, the Lord your God, am a jealous God, visiting the iniquity of the fathers upon the children to the third and fourth generations of those who hate Me, 6 but showing mercy to thousands, to those who love Me and keep My commandments.

Ephesians 4:22-24 **22** that you put off, concerning your former conduct, the old man which grows corrupt according to the deceitful lusts, **23** and be renewed in the spirit of your mind, **24** and that you put on the new man which was created according to God, in true righteousness and holiness.

Isaiah 14:12-14 - **12** "How you are fallen from heaven, O Lucifer, son of the morning! How you are cut down to the ground, You who weakened the nations! **13** For you have said in your heart: 'I will ascend into heaven, I will exalt my throne above the stars of God; I will also sit on the mount of the congregation On the farthest sides of the north; **14** I will ascend above the heights of the clouds, I will be like the Most High.'

Romans 12:2 - Do not conform to the pattern of this world, but be transformed by the renewing of your mind. Then you will be able to test and approve what God's will is—his good, pleasing and perfect will.

2 Timothy 2:15 - 15 Study and do your best to present yourself to God approved, a workman [tested by trial] who has no reason to be ashamed, accurately handling and skillfully teaching the word of truth.

Psalm 115:4 - Their idols are silver and gold, The work of men's hands

Daniel 4:28-32 - **28** All this came upon King Nebuchadnezzar. **29** At the end of the twelve months he was walking about the royal palace of Babylon. **30** The king spoke, saying, "Is not this great Babylon, that I have built for a royal dwelling by my mighty power and for the honor of my majesty?"

31 While the word was still in the king's mouth, a voice fell from heaven: "King Nebuchadnezzar, to you it is spoken: the kingdom has departed from you! **32** And they shall drive you from men, and your dwelling shall be with the beasts of the field. They shall make you eat grass like oxen; and seven times shall pass over you, until you know that the Most High rules in the kingdom of men, and gives it to whomever He chooses."

2 Chronicles 7:14 - if My people who are called by My name will humble themselves, and pray and seek My face, and turn from their wicked ways, then I will hear from heaven, and will forgive their sin and heal their land.

2 Corinthians 6:16 - 16 What agreement is there between the temple of God and idols? For we are the temple of the living God. As God has said: "I will live with them and walk among them, and I will be their God, and they will be my people."

Conclusion

Romans 8:1 - Therefore, there is now no condemnation for those who are in Christ Jesus,

Resources

Barboza, D., & Warren, A. (2002, February 25). At Enron, Lavish Excess Often Came Before Success. Retrieved August 17, 2014

"Cats in the Cradle" Artist: Harry Chapin, Album: Verities & Balderdash, Released: 1974

Johnson, B. T. (2016). Pharisees. In J. D. Barry, D. Bomar, D. R. Brown, R. Klippenstein, D. Mangum, C. Sinclair Wolcott, … W. Widder (Eds.), The Lexham Bible Dictionary. Bellingham, WA: Lexham Press

Jones, T. H. (1996). David. In D. R. W. Wood, I. H. Marshall, A. R. Millard, J. I. Packer, & D. J. Wiseman (Eds.), New Bible dictionary (3rd ed., p. 260). Leicester, England; Downers Grove, IL: InterVarsity Press

Knox, D. B. (1996). Wealth. In D. R. W. Wood, I. H. Marshall, A. R. Millard, J. I. Packer, & D. J. Wiseman (Eds.), New Bible dictionary (3rd ed., p. 1233). Leicester, England; Downers Grove, IL: InterVarsity Press

Mallon, B. (2013, July 12). Divorce Study: Financial Arguments Early In Relationship May Predict Divorce. Retrieved August 17, 2014, from http://www.huffingtonpost.com/2013/07/12/divorce-study_n_3587811.html

Manser, M. H. (2009). Dictionary of Bible Themes: The Accessible and Comprehensive Tool for Topical Studies. London: Martin Manser

Matthew Henry's Commentary; Chapter 6:6-12

Prison, Prisoners and the Bible, A Paper Delivered to "Breaking Down the Walls Conference" by Dr Christopher D. Marshall* Tyndale Graduate School of Theology, Auckland retrieved from
http://www.restorativejustice.org/10fulltext/marshall-christopher.-prison-prisoners-and-the-bible/

The Only Definition of Success That Matters, by Jeff Haden, July 28, 2012, retrieved from http://www.inc.com/jeff-haden/the-only-definition-of-success-that-matters.html

The Sermon on the Mount, By: Brian Schwertley, retrieved from http://www.reformedonline.com/view/reformedonline/sermononmount1.htm

Read more at
http://www.brainyquote.com/citation/quotes/quotes/s/samuelbutl122806.html#eo0f4GIOMo6fcYht.99

Samuel Butler. (n.d.). BrainyQuote.com. Retrieved August 17, 2014, from BrainyQuote.com Web site: http://www.brainyquote.com/quotes/quotes/s/samuelbutl122806.html

Source: Israel Ministry of Foreign Affairs, Copyright 2012 The American-Israeli Cooperative
Enterprise retrieved from
http://www.jewishvirtuallibrary.org/jsource/History/Romans.html

Wall Street (1987), Director: Oliver Stone, Writers: Stanley Weiser, Oliver Stone

www.ingramcontent.com/pod-product-compliance
Lightning Source LLC
Chambersburg PA
CBHW060757090426
42736CB00002B/57